CR
6/13

SUPER COMMA SAVES THE DAY!

By Nadia Higgins • Illustrated by Mernie Gallagher-Cole

The Child's World®

Published by The Child's World®
1980 Lookout Drive • Mankato, MN 56003-1705
800-599-READ • www.childsworld.com

Acknowledgments
The Child's World®: Mary Berendes, Publishing Director
The Design Lab: Design and production
Red Line Editorial: Editorial direction

Design elements: Billyfoto/Dreamstime;
Dan Ionut Popescu/Dreamstime

ISBN 9781614732679
LCCN 2012932873

Printed in the United States of America
Mankato, MN
July 2012
PA02117

About the Author: Nadia Higgins is a children's book author based in Minneapolis, Minnesota. Nadia has been a punctuation fan since the age of five, when she first wrote "Happy Birthday!" on a homemade card. "I love punctuation because it is both orderly and expressive," Nadia says. Her dream is to visit Punctuation Junction someday.

About the Illustrator: Mernie Gallagher-Cole is a freelance children's book illustrator living outside of Philadelphia. She has illustrated many children's books. Mernie enjoys punctuation marks so much that she uses a hyphen in her last name!

My name is Super Comma. I am a comma. I break up sentences to make them easier to understand.
Pause a little when you read a comma.

Giggle, giggle, snort, squeal. The commas of Punctuation Junction tittered with excitement. Today was Halloween. And the squirmy punctuation had outdone themselves once again.

They were dressed up as a school of fish. Their leader, Super Comma, was a shark. "Snap!" She pretended to attack them.

Giggle, GIGGLE, snort, SQUEAL. The commas laughed so hard they swirled in the air.

"Come on, everybody!" Super Comma called. And the commas wriggled out into the dark night.

Noises were everywhere.

Whooooooo. An owl hooted.

Arrrr-ooooooo. A dog howled.

VARRRROOOOOOM. What was that?

A pencil-thin mummy jumped out from behind the bushes. Was that a leaf blower in his hands?

"Tricky trick!" he said with an evil laugh. Then, *WHOOOOOOOOSH!* A blast of air sent the commas spinning out of sight.

The commas were missing! This looked like a job for a superhero.
Super Comma shot into town to find her friends.
Oh, no! She saw that a comma was needed right away.

Zap! Super Comma used her comma power to set things straight.

Time to eat, kids!

The comma shows that she is talking to the kids, not about them.

Super Comma sped on. Things were not looking clearer at her next stop. Mary's interview was all wrong without commas.

Zap!
Super Comma
saved the
show.

I love reading, movies, cooking, cats, and gardening.

The superhero arrived just in time at Pam's house.

Super Comma found a comma at the mall. But the dazed, dizzy punctuation was lost.

Another lost comma was causing trouble at the gym.

Hang on Grandma, and I will be right there.

Poof! With an "and" and the comma moved, the sentence was fixed!

Just then, Super Comma heard yelling outside.
Oh, no! Evil Pete was getting away! And a stray
comma was to blame!

Zap! Zing! Zow-ow-ow! Super Comma to the rescue!

Without the comma, there's one clear idea: Snatch that villain!

Don't let him get away!

The police led Evil Pete away to jail. Things became much easier to understand in the town.

"Over here, commas!" Super Comma called out. The commas all came back. They took their places once again.

"You saved the day, Super Comma!" everyone cheered. What a happy Halloween it was in Punctuation Junction.

PUNCTUATION FUN

Practice reading these sentences out loud. Where does it feel like you should pause? Chances are, that is where a comma needs to go. Where would you put commas in these sentences? The number at the end tells you how many commas are missing.

1. You like pizza don't you? (1)

2. Please bring me my coffee slippers and phone. (2)

3. Hey Super Comma come look at this. (1)

4. It has been a long hard day. (1)

5. Once upon a time there was a princess who fell in love with punctuation. (1)

6. As I said a shark is a kind of fish. (1)

DO NOT WRITE IN THE BOOK!

FUN FACTS

The Hardest One

Look in a grammar book. You will see that commas get more pages than any other kind of punctuation. Commas have the most rules. And they are hardest to use. Even punctuation experts do not agree about how to use commas.

Math Power

Commas come in handy with big numbers. Starting at the ones column, use a comma after every third number.

Turn It Around

In English, we read from left to right. Arabic speakers read from right to left. Everything is turned around—including commas. In Arabic, a comma looks like this: '.

Dear Comma,

Commas also come in handy when you are writing a letter. Use a comma after Dear and the person's name. Use a comma after your goodbye word, too.

A Date to Remember

You should find a comma in every date that includes the month, day, and year. The little squiggle goes after the day and before the year as January 1, 2077.